# The UNITED STATES PRESIDENTS

# ★ ★ George H.W. ★ ★

# BUSH

## Heidi M.D. Elston

**Big Buddy Books**

An Imprint of Abdo Publishing
abdopublishing.com

# abdopublishing.com

Published by Abdo Publishing, a division of ABDO, PO Box 398166, Minneapolis, Minnesota 55439.
Copyright © 2017 by Abdo Consulting Group, Inc. International copyrights reserved in all countries. No part of this book may be reproduced in any form without written permission from the publisher. Big Buddy Books™ is a trademark and logo of Abdo Publishing.

Printed in the United States of America, North Mankato, Minnesota
062016
092016

 THIS BOOK CONTAINS
RECYCLED MATERIALS

Design: Sarah DeYoung, Mighty Media, Inc.
Production: Mighty Media, Inc.
Editor: Paige Polinsky
Cover Photograph: Getty Images
Interior Photographs: AP Images (pp. 7, 19); Corbis (pp. 27, 29); George Bush Presidential Library and
     Museum (pp. 5, 6, 7, 9, 11, 13, 15, 17, 21, 23, 25)

**Cataloging-in-Publication Data**

Names: Elston, Heidi M.D., author.
Title: George H.W. Bush / by Heidi M.D. Elston.
Description: Minneapolis, MN : Abdo Publishing, [2017] | Series: United States
     presidents | Includes bibliographical references and index.
Identifiers: LCCN 2015957274 | ISBN 9781680780857 (lib. bdg.) |
     ISBN 9781680775051 (ebook)
Subjects: LCSH: Bush, George H.W. (George Herbert Walker), 1924- --Juvenile
     literature. | Presidents--United States--Biography--Juvenile literature. |
     United States--Politics and government--1989-1993--Juvenile literature.
Classification: DDC 973.931/092 [B]--dc23
LC record available at http://lccn.loc.gov/2015957274

# Contents

# George H.W. Bush

George H.W. Bush was the forty-first US president. Before he was president, Bush was a US Navy pilot, business owner, and congressman. Through the 1970s, he served as a US **ambassador**. He also directed the **CIA**.

Bush became vice president under **Republican** Ronald Reagan in 1981. Eight years later, Bush became president. Bush helped reduce the world's **nuclear weapons**. He led the United States through the **Persian Gulf War**. Today, he remains active in community service.

# Timeline

**1924**

On June 12, George Herbert Walker Bush was born in Milton, Massachusetts.

**1966**

Bush was elected to the US House of **Representatives**.

**1943**

Bush became a US Navy pilot.

**1973**

Bush became chairman of the **Republican National Committee**.

## 1981

On January 20, Bush became vice president under Ronald Reagan.

## 1989

Bush became the forty-first US president on January 20.

## 1991

The **Persian Gulf War** began and ended.

## 2010

Bush received the Presidential Medal of Freedom.

# Early Life

George Herbert Walker Bush was born on June 12, 1924, in Milton, Massachusetts. George's parents were Prescott and Dorothy Bush. Their family soon moved to Connecticut.

In 1937, George began school in Massachusetts. He played baseball and soccer. George **graduated** in 1942.

★ FAST FACTS ★

**Born:** June 12, 1924

**Wife:** Barbara Pierce (1925–)

**Children:** six

**Political Party:** Republican

**Age at Inauguration:** 64

**Years Served:** 1989–1993

**Vice President:** Dan Quayle

George (*right*) with his sister, Nancy. Because George shared his snacks, his family called him "Have Half."

# War Hero

Bush wanted to fight in **World War II**. So, in 1943, he became a US Navy pilot. His plane was shot down the next year. Bush was honored for his bravery. He soon returned home.

In 1945, Bush married Barbara Pierce. He also left the navy. Bush entered Yale University in Connecticut to study **economics**.

Bush and Barbara's son George Walker was born in 1946. After Bush **graduated** in 1948, he moved his family to Texas. There, he worked for an oil company.

At 18 years old, Bush was the youngest pilot in the US Navy.

# Striking It Rich

In 1950, Bush and Barbara welcomed daughter Robin. The next year, Bush helped start a new oil company. He became very wealthy.

Bush and Barbara's son John "Jeb" Ellis was born in 1953. Sadly, Robin died that same year. The Bushes later had three more children.

In 1964, Bush ran for the US Senate. He lost. But in 1966, he was elected to the US House of **Representatives**. Bush again ran for the US Senate in 1970. Once more, he lost.

The Bush family

# Working in Politics

President Richard Nixon made Bush US **ambassador** to the **United Nations** in 1971. The next year, the Watergate **scandal** was revealed. **Republicans** had paid burglars to steal secrets from **Democratic** offices. Nixon took part in it.

In 1973, Bush became chairman of the **Republican National Committee**. Nixon left office on August 7, 1974. Vice President Gerald Ford became president. Ford made Bush the **CIA** director in 1976. Bush quit when Democrat Jimmy Carter became president in 1977.

Bush (*right*) stood behind President Nixon during Watergate.

# Vice President

Bush ran for president in 1979. However, the **Republican** Party selected Ronald Reagan. Reagan asked Bush to run as his vice president.

In 1980, Reagan beat Jimmy Carter. Reagan and Bush entered office on January 20, 1981. They were reelected in 1984. As Vice President, Bush led several crime **task forces**.

The next presidential election took place in 1988. The Republicans selected Bush for president. He won the election on November 8, 1988.

During Bush's presidential campaign, he called for "a kinder, gentler nation."

# President Bush

On January 20, 1989, Bush became the forty-first US president. That March, he handled a terrible event. A huge ship spilled oil into Prince William Sound, Alaska. Bush sent government teams to lead the cleanup.

Bush soon had a new challenge. Panama's leader, Manuel Noriega, was dealing drugs. In December, Bush sent troops into Panama. Noriega gave himself up.

**SUPREME COURT APPOINTMENTS**

**David H. Souter:** 1990

**Clarence Thomas:** 1991

Bush's vice president, Dan Quayle, was a senator from Indiana.

# War in the Gulf

In 1990, Iraq's leader, Saddam Hussein, invaded Kuwait. World leaders feared Iraq would invade more countries.

Bush sent troops to protect Saudi Arabia. He united other countries against Iraq. They demanded that Iraq withdraw. Hussein refused.

On January 16, 1991, the United States led an attack on Iraq. This began the **Persian Gulf War**. The United States led another attack on February 24. But four days later, Bush ended the attack. The war was over.

President Bush visited US troops stationed in the Middle East.

# Peace and Unrest

Bush next focused on the Soviet Union. In 1991, he signed an agreement with Soviet president Mikhail Gorbachev. It reduced the **nuclear weapons** in both countries.

In 1992, Bush faced problems at home. African-American Rodney King was attacked by white police officers. A camera had recorded the crime. But the officers were not punished.

This decision started **riots** in Los Angeles. Fifty-three people died. Bush sent armed forces to control the city.

# PRESIDENT BUSH'S CABINET

President Bush and Vice President Quayle (*center*) with the cabinet in 1992

## January 20, 1989–January 20, 1993

★ **STATE:** James A. Baker III

★ **TREASURY:** Nicholas F. Brady

★ **ATTORNEY GENERAL:** Dick Thornburgh, William P. Barr (from November 20, 1991)

★ **INTERIOR:** Manuel Lujan Jr.

★ **AGRICULTURE:** Clayton K. Yeutter, Edward Madigan (from March 7, 1991)

★ **COMMERCE:** Robert A. Mosbacher

★ **LABOR:** Elizabeth H. Dole

★ **DEFENSE:** Dick Cheney

★ **HEALTH AND HUMAN SERVICES:** Louis W. Sullivan

★ **HOUSING AND URBAN DEVELOPMENT:** Jack Kemp

★ **TRANSPORTATION:** Samuel K. Skinner, Andrew H. Card (from January 22, 1992)

★ **ENERGY:** James D. Watkins

★ **EDUCATION:** Lauro F. Cavazos Jr., Lamar Alexander (from March 14, 1991)

★ **VETERANS AFFAIRS:** Edward J. Derwinski (from March 15, 1989)

# Election Defeat

In August 1992, **Republicans** chose Bush for reelection. But the US **economy** was weak. Jobs were hard to find. Many people blamed President Bush.

**Democrats** chose Arkansas governor Bill Clinton for president. Texas businessman Ross Perot ran without a **political** party.

On November 3, 1992, Americans cast their votes. Many Republicans voted for Perot instead of Bush. Because of this, Bush didn't get enough votes to beat Clinton.

Bush gracefully accepted defeat. He said, "The people have spoken."

# Home to Houston

On January 20, 1993, Bush and his wife returned to Houston, Texas. There, Bush spent time with his family.

Two of Bush's sons have followed in their father's footsteps. George W. became the forty-third US president. He won reelection in 2004.

Jeb became Florida's governor in 1998. He was reelected in 2002. And on June 15, 2015, Jeb joined the 2016 presidential race. But he did not do well. Jeb left the race on February 20, 2016.

Bush has enjoyed watching his sons George W. (*center*) and Jeb (*right*) succeed in politics.

# A Leader Again

After leaving office, Bush continued to serve. In 2004, a **tsunami** hit several Asian and African countries. Millions were left homeless. Together, Bush and former president Clinton raised money for the survivors. They did the same for victims of **Hurricane** Katrina in 2005.

In 2010, President Barack Obama awarded Bush the Presidential Medal of Freedom for his service. As president, George H.W. Bush showed strong leadership. He worked to make America a kinder and gentler nation.

Bush visited tsunami survivors to encourage those who were suffering.

# Office of the President

## Branches of Government

The US government has three branches. They are the executive, legislative, and judicial branches. Each branch has some power over the others. This is called a system of checks and balances.

### ★ Executive Branch

The executive branch enforces laws. It is made up of the president, the vice president, and the president's cabinet. The president represents the United States around the world. He or she also signs bills into law and leads the military.

### ★ Legislative Branch

The legislative branch makes laws, maintains the military, and regulates trade. It also has the power to declare war. This branch includes the Senate and the House of Representatives. Together, these two houses form Congress.

### ★ Judicial Branch

The judicial branch interprets laws. It is made up of district courts, courts of appeals, and the Supreme Court. District courts try cases. Sometimes people disagree with a trial's outcome. Then he or she may appeal. If a court of appeals supports the ruling, a person may appeal to the Supreme Court.

# Qualifications for Office

To be president, a candidate must be at least 35 years old. The person must be a natural-born US citizen. He or she must also have lived in the United States for at least 14 years.

# Electoral College

The US presidential election is an indirect election. Voters from each state choose electors. These electors represent their state in the Electoral College. Each elector has one electoral vote. Electors cast their vote for the candidate with the highest number of votes from people in their state. A candidate must receive the majority of Electoral College votes to win.

# Term of Office

Each president may be elected to two four-year terms. The presidential election is held on the Tuesday after the first Monday in November. The president is sworn in on January 20 of the following year. At that time, he or she takes the oath of office.
It states:

> I do solemnly swear (or affirm) that I will faithfully execute the office of President of the United States, and will to the best of my ability, preserve, protect and defend the Constitution of the United States.

31

# Line of Succession

The Presidential Succession Act of 1947 states who becomes president if the president cannot serve. The vice president is first in the line. Next are the Speaker of the House and the President Pro Tempore of the Senate. It may happen that none of these individuals is able to serve. Then the office falls to the president's cabinet members. They would take office in the order in which each department was created:

Secretary of State

Secretary of the Treasury

Secretary of Defense

Attorney General

Secretary of the Interior

Secretary of Agriculture

Secretary of Commerce

Secretary of Labor

Secretary of Health and Human Services

Secretary of Housing and Urban Development

Secretary of Transportation

Secretary of Energy

Secretary of Education

Secretary of Veterans Affairs

Secretary of Homeland Security

# Benefits

★ While in office, the president receives a salary. It is $400,000 per year. He or she lives in the White House. The president also has 24-hour Secret Service protection.

★ The president may travel on a Boeing 747 jet. This special jet is called Air Force One. It can hold 70 passengers. It has kitchens, a dining room, sleeping areas, and more. Air Force One can fly halfway around the world before needing to refuel. It can even refuel in flight!

★ When the president travels by car, he or she uses Cadillac One. It is a Cadillac Deville that has been modified. The car has heavy armor and communications systems. The president may even take Cadillac One along when visiting other countries.

★ The president also travels on a helicopter. It is called Marine One. It may also be taken along when the president visits other countries.

★ Sometimes the president needs to get away with family and friends. Camp David is the official presidential retreat. It is located in Maryland. The US Navy maintains the retreat. The US Marine Corps keeps it secure. The camp offers swimming, tennis, golf, and hiking.

★ When the president leaves office, he or she receives lifetime Secret Service protection. He or she also receives a yearly pension of $203,700. The former president also receives money for office space, supplies, and staff.

# PRESIDENTS AND THEIR TERMS

| PRESIDENT | PARTY | TOOK OFFICE | LEFT OFFICE | TERMS SERVED | VICE PRESIDENT |
|---|---|---|---|---|---|
| George Washington | None | April 30, 1789 | March 4, 1797 | Two | John Adams |
| John Adams | Federalist | March 4, 1797 | March 4, 1801 | One | Thomas Jefferson |
| Thomas Jefferson | Democratic-Republican | March 4, 1801 | March 4, 1809 | Two | Aaron Burr, George Clinton |
| James Madison | Democratic-Republican | March 4, 1809 | March 4, 1817 | Two | George Clinton, Elbridge Gerry |
| James Monroe | Democratic-Republican | March 4, 1817 | March 4, 1825 | Two | Daniel D. Tompkins |
| John Quincy Adams | Democratic-Republican | March 4, 1825 | March 4, 1829 | One | John C. Calhoun |
| Andrew Jackson | Democrat | March 4, 1829 | March 4, 1837 | Two | John C. Calhoun, Martin Van Buren |
| Martin Van Buren | Democrat | March 4, 1837 | March 4, 1841 | One | Richard M. Johnson |
| William H. Harrison | Whig | March 4, 1841 | April 4, 1841 | Died During First Term | John Tyler |
| John Tyler | Whig | April 6, 1841 | March 4, 1845 | Completed Harrison's Term | Office Vacant |
| James K. Polk | Democrat | March 4, 1845 | March 4, 1849 | One | George M. Dallas |
| Zachary Taylor | Whig | March 5, 1849 | July 9, 1850 | Died During First Term | Millard Fillmore |

| PRESIDENT | PARTY | TOOK OFFICE | LEFT OFFICE | TERMS SERVED | VICE PRESIDENT |
|---|---|---|---|---|---|
| **Millard Fillmore** | Whig | July 10, 1850 | March 4, 1853 | Completed Taylor's Term | Office Vacant |
| **Franklin Pierce** | Democrat | March 4, 1853 | March 4, 1857 | One | William R.D. King |
| **James Buchanan** | Democrat | March 4, 1857 | March 4, 1861 | One | John C. Breckinridge |
| **Abraham Lincoln** | Republican | March 4, 1861 | April 15, 1865 | Served One Term, Died During Second Term | Hannibal Hamlin, Andrew Johnson |
| **Andrew Johnson** | Democrat | April 15, 1865 | March 4, 1869 | Completed Lincoln's Second Term | Office Vacant |
| **Ulysses S. Grant** | Republican | March 4, 1869 | March 4, 1877 | Two | Schuyler Colfax, Henry Wilson |
| **Rutherford B. Hayes** | Republican | March 3, 1877 | March 4, 1881 | One | William A. Wheeler |
| **James A. Garfield** | Republican | March 4, 1881 | September 19, 1881 | Died During First Term | Chester Arthur |
| **Chester Arthur** | Republican | September 20, 1881 | March 4, 1885 | Completed Garfield's Term | Office Vacant |
| **Grover Cleveland** | Democrat | March 4, 1885 | March 4, 1889 | One | Thomas A. Hendricks |
| **Benjamin Harrison** | Republican | March 4, 1889 | March 4, 1893 | One | Levi P. Morton |
| **Grover Cleveland** | Democrat | March 4, 1893 | March 4, 1897 | One | Adlai E. Stevenson |
| **William McKinley** | Republican | March 4, 1897 | September 14, 1901 | Served One Term, Died During Second Term | Garret A. Hobart, Theodore Roosevelt |

| PRESIDENT | PARTY | TOOK OFFICE | LEFT OFFICE | TERMS SERVED | VICE PRESIDENT |
| --- | --- | --- | --- | --- | --- |
| Theodore Roosevelt | Republican | September 14, 1901 | March 4, 1909 | Completed McKinley's Second Term, Served One Term | Office Vacant, Charles Fairbanks |
| William Taft | Republican | March 4, 1909 | March 4, 1913 | One | James S. Sherman |
| Woodrow Wilson | Democrat | March 4, 1913 | March 4, 1921 | Two | Thomas R. Marshall |
| Warren G. Harding | Republican | March 4, 1921 | August 2, 1923 | Died During First Term | Calvin Coolidge |
| Calvin Coolidge | Republican | August 3, 1923 | March 4, 1929 | Completed Harding's Term, Served One Term | Office Vacant, Charles Dawes |
| Herbert Hoover | Republican | March 4, 1929 | March 4, 1933 | One | Charles Curtis |
| Franklin D. Roosevelt | Democrat | March 4, 1933 | April 12, 1945 | Served Three Terms, Died During Fourth Term | John Nance Garner, Henry A. Wallace, Harry S. Truman |
| Harry S. Truman | Democrat | April 12, 1945 | January 20, 1953 | Completed Roosevelt's Fourth Term, Served One Term | Office Vacant, Alben Barkley |
| Dwight D. Eisenhower | Republican | January 20, 1953 | January 20, 1961 | Two | Richard Nixon |
| John F. Kennedy | Democrat | January 20, 1961 | November 22, 1963 | Died During First Term | Lyndon B. Johnson |
| Lyndon B. Johnson | Democrat | November 22, 1963 | January 20, 1969 | Completed Kennedy's Term, Served One Term | Office Vacant, Hubert H. Humphrey |
| Richard Nixon | Republican | January 20, 1969 | August 9, 1974 | Completed First Term, Resigned During Second Term | Spiro T. Agnew, Gerald Ford |

| PRESIDENT | PARTY | TOOK OFFICE | LEFT OFFICE | TERMS SERVED | VICE PRESIDENT |
|---|---|---|---|---|---|
| Gerald Ford | Republican | August 9, 1974 | January 20, 1977 | Completed Nixon's Second Term | Nelson A. Rockefeller |
| Jimmy Carter | Democrat | January 20, 1977 | January 20, 1981 | One | Walter Mondale |
| Ronald Reagan | Republican | January 20, 1981 | January 20, 1989 | Two | George H.W. Bush |
| George H.W. Bush | Republican | January 20, 1989 | January 20, 1993 | One | Dan Quayle |
| Bill Clinton | Democrat | January 20, 1993 | January 20, 2001 | Two | Al Gore |
| George W. Bush | Republican | January 20, 2001 | January 20, 2009 | Two | Dick Cheney |
| Barack Obama | Democrat | January 20, 2009 | January 20, 2017 | Two | Joe Biden |

"This is America . . . a brilliant diversity spread like stars, like a thousand points of light in a broad and peaceful sky." George H.W. Bush

## ★ WRITE TO THE PRESIDENT ★

**You may write to the president at:**
The White House
1600 Pennsylvania Avenue NW
Washington, DC 20500

**You may e-mail the president at:**
comments@whitehouse.gov

37

# Glossary

**ambassador**—the job of speaking for, or representing, one country to other countries.

**CIA**—Central Intelligence Agency. A US government agency that gathers information about foreign nations to help protect US national security.

**Democrat**—a member of the Democratic political party.

**economy**—the way that a country produces, sells, and buys goods and services. The study of this is called economics.

**graduate** (GRA-juh-wayt)—to complete a level of schooling.

**hurricane**—a tropical storm that forms over seawater with strong winds, rain, thunder, and lightning.

**nuclear weapon**—a weapon that uses the power created by splitting atoms.

**Persian Gulf War**—a war fought between Iraq and many countries, including the United States, in 1991.

**political**—the art or science of government. Something referring to politics is political. A person who is active in politics is a politician.

**representative**—someone chosen in an election to act or speak for the people who voted for him or her.

**Republican**—a member of the Republican political party.

**Republican National Committee**—a group that provides leadership for the Republican Party.

**riot**—sometimes violent disorder caused by a large group of people.

**scandal**—an action that shocks people and disgraces those connected with it.

**task force**—a group organized for a short time to perform a specific task.

**tsunami** (soo-NAH-mee)—a group of powerful ocean waves that can destroy areas.

**United Nations**—a group of nations formed in 1945. Its goals are peace, human rights, security, and social and economic development.

**World War II**—a war fought in Europe, Asia, and Africa from 1939 to 1945.

★ **WEBSITES** ★

To learn more about the US Presidents, visit **booklinks.abdopublishing.com**. These links are routinely monitored and updated to provide the most current information available.

# Index